Community Helpers

Auto Mechanics

by Tracey Boraas

Consultant:
Carl D. Miller
Chairman of the Board
Automotive Service Association

Bridgestone Books
an imprint of Capstone Press
Mankato, Minnesota

Bridgestone Books are published by Capstone Press
151 Good Counsel Drive, P.O. Box 669, Mankato, Minnesota 56002
http://www.capstone-press.com

Library of Congress Cataloging-in-Publication Data
Boraas, Tracey.
    Auto Mechanics/by Tracey Boraas
    p. cm.—(Community helpers)
    Includes bibliographical references and index.
    Summary: Explains what auto mechanics do; describes their uniforms, tools, and places
of work; and indicates the training and education needed for the job.
    ISBN 0-7368-0072-7
    1. Automobile mechanics—Juvenile literature. 2. Automobiles—Maintenance and
repair—Vocational guidance—Juvenile literature. [1. Automobile mechanics.
    2. Automobiles—Maintenance and repair. 3. Occupations.] I. Title. II. Series: Community
Helpers (Mankato, Minn.)
TL152.B615   1999
629.28'72—dc21   98-179161
                                                        CIP
                                                        AC

Editorial Credits
Michael Fallon, editor; James Franklin, cover designer; Sheri Gosewisch, photo researcher

Photo Credits
Automotive Service Excellence, 4
Don Franklin, 8
Leslie O'Shaughnessy, 14
Photo Network/Tom Campbell, 6; Stephen Saks, 12; Douglas Pulsipher, 16
Steve C. Healey, 10
Unicorn Stock Photos/A. Rodham, cover; Jeff Greenberg, 18, 20

Table of Contents

Auto Mechanics

Auto mechanics work on cars and trucks. Mechanics look for broken parts and fix them. Mechanics also replace old parts with new parts. They help people keep their cars and trucks running.

What Auto Mechanics Do

Auto mechanics fix the engines that power cars and trucks. Mechanics put in new engine parts and new brakes. They change tires and headlights. Headlights are lights on the front of cars or trucks.

What Auto Mechanics Wear

Auto mechanics' clothes become dirty at work. Most auto mechanics wear uniforms that are easy to clean. Some mechanics wear coveralls. This one-piece suit of clothing fits over clothes to keep them clean.

Tools Auto Mechanics Use

Auto mechanics use screwdrivers and wrenches. They tighten and loosen parts with these tools. Mechanics also use electric power tools to fix engine parts. These tools need electricity to work.

Kinds of Auto Mechanics

Auto mechanics do different kinds of jobs. Some mechanics work on many kinds of cars or trucks. Others work on only one kind. They may fix only racing cars or school buses.

Where Auto Mechanics Work

Most auto mechanics fix cars and trucks at repair garages. Many places that sell cars and trucks have repair garages. Gas stations also may have repair garages.

Auto Mechanics and School

Many people go to vocational schools to become mechanics. Vocational schools are where people learn a trade. Students practice fixing cars and trucks at vocational schools. Some people learn to be auto mechanics from other mechanics.

People Who Help Auto Mechanics

Auto mechanics need help from other people. Mechanics often help one another work on cars and trucks. Each mechanic may fix a different part of an engine. Parts shop workers send mechanics the parts they need.

How Auto Mechanics Help Others

Auto mechanics help people keep their cars and trucks running. They fix cars and trucks that break down. Auto mechanics answer people's questions about their cars and trucks. They help people learn how their cars and trucks work.

Hands on: Learn How Grease Works

Some car or truck parts rub together. The rubbing can cause the parts to wear out. Auto mechanics put grease on these parts. Grease is thick oil that makes parts move more easily. You can learn how grease works.

What You Need

Two pieces of sandpaper
Petroleum jelly

What You Do

1. Rub the rough sides of two pieces of sandpaper together.
2. Notice how hard it is to move the sandpaper back and forth.
3. Coat the rough side of one piece of sandpaper with petroleum jelly.
4. Rub the coated side of the sandpaper against the other piece of sandpaper.
5. Notice how easy it is to move the paper back and forth now. You have learned how auto mechanics use grease to keep parts moving easily.

Words to Know

coverall (CUH-vur-awl)—a one-piece suit of clothing that fits over other clothes

repair garage (ri-PAIR guh-RAHJ)—a place where people fix cars and trucks

screwdriver (SKROO-drye-vur)—a tool that tightens or loosens screws

vocational school (voh-KAY-shuhn-uhl SKOOL)—a place where people learn a trade

wrench (RENCH)—a tool that tightens or loosens parts

Read More

Florian, Douglas. *An Auto Mechanic.* How We Work. New York: Mulberry Books, 1994.

Oxlade, Chris. *Car.* Take It Apart! Parsippany, N.J.: Silver Press, 1996.

Internet Sites

Automotive Learning On-Line

http://www.innerbody.com/innerauto/htm/auto.html

Cars and Stuff

http://www.ipl.org/youth/Cars

Index